STAR
TREK
LIVES!

Star Trek premiered on September 8, 1966, and ran for just three seasons, a total of seventy-nine episodes. The final episode aired on June 3, 1969. Ten years later, *Star Trek: The Motion Picture* was released. Trekkies were delighted. More movies followed. Fans can't seem to get enough of Captain Kirk, Mr. Spock, or the *Enterprise*.

Many of today's fans weren't even born when the TV show first aired, but it doesn't seem to matter. Trekkies are a loyal and dedicated bunch, responsible for keeping Star Trek in the hearts and minds of millions of people. In their words: STAR TREK LIVES!

Books by Daniel Cohen

GHOSTLY TERRORS
THE GREATEST MONSTERS IN THE WORLD
HORROR IN THE MOVIES
THE MONSTERS OF STAR TREK
MONSTERS YOU NEVER HEARD OF
REAL GHOSTS
SCIENCE FICTION'S GREATEST MONSTERS
STRANGE AND AMAZING FACTS ABOUT STAR TREK
SUPERMONSTERS
THE WORLD'S MOST FAMOUS GHOSTS

Books by Daniel and Susan Cohen

HEROES OF THE CHALLENGER
THE KID'S GUIDE TO HOME COMPUTERS
ROCK VIDEO SUPERSTARS
WRESTLING SUPERSTARS
WRESTLING SUPERSTARS II

Available from ARCHWAY paperbacks

STRANGE &
·AMAZING·
FACTS ABOUT

STAR
TREK®

DANIEL COHEN

illustrated with photos

AN ARCHWAY PAPERBACK
Published by POCKET BOOKS • NEW YORK

AN ARCHWAY PAPERBACK *Original*

 An Archway Paperback published by
POCKET BOOKS, a division of Simon & Schuster, Inc.
1230 Avenue of the Americas, New York, N.Y. 10020

This book is an Archway Paperback published by Pocket
Books, a division of Simon & Schuster, Inc. Under Exclusive
License from Paramount Pictures Corporation, The Trade-
mark Owner.

ISBN: 0-671-63014-8

First Archway Paperback printing December, 1986

10 9 8 7 6 5 4 3 2 1

For
Pamela Moore
Epstein

Contents

STRANGE &
· AMAZING ·
FACTS ABOUT

STAR
TREK®

Chapter 1

THE HISTORY OF STAR TREK

The full text of the message spoken at the beginning of each episode of Star Trek is:

"Space—the final frontier. These are the voyages of the starship *Enterprise*. Its five-year mission: to explore strange new worlds; to seek out new life and new civilizations; to boldly go where no man has gone before."

The original Star Trek television series was the creation of writer and producer Gene Roddenberry. It premiered at 8:30 Thursday evening, September 8, 1966, on NBC television, and ran for three seasons, a total of seventy-nine episodes.

The cast of Star Trek remained remarkably stable over the years. However, in the first pilot episode of the series, which was called "The Cage" and was filmed in 1964, the captain of

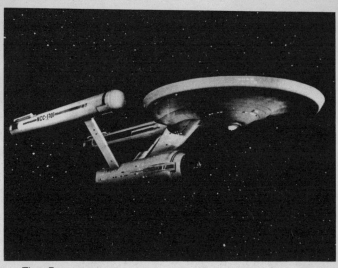

The *Enterprise*

the *Enterprise* was not James T. Kirk, played by William Shatner, but Christopher Pike, played by Jeffrey Hunter. This pilot was later turned into the two-part episode called "The Menagerie," broadcast halfway through the show's first season.

After viewing the pilot, NBC executives liked it well enough, but suggested that Roddenberry get rid of one of the characters, Mr. Spock. Though at the time no one could have predicted how important Spock would become to the show, Roddenberry insisted on keeping him in, because he thought it was nice to have an alien on board the *Enterprise*. A second pilot was made, entitled "Where No Man Has Gone Before" and this was the one that really sold the show to the NBC executives. It became the third Star Trek episode actually broadcast. The first Star Trek episode to be aired was "The Man Trap," which was the sixth to be made.

Though the series quickly developed a large and loyal following, Star Trek was never a great favorite of network executives. It was a fairly expensive show to produce, and it didn't have the high ratings of a real hit show. Today the TV ratings systems are a little different. The networks are not merely interested in how many people have the TV set turned on, they want to know who is actually watching the show and how much he or she is enjoying it. By today's standards, Star Trek would be considered a hit. It was pretty sophisticated, and the executives felt viewers couldn't understand it. Star Trek ran two more years, and each year NBC announced plans to cancel it. It was then that the TV executives, and indeed the Star Trek cast, discovered just how many loyal fans the show really did have. Letters demanding the show be kept on the air flooded NBC, and the second time there may have been over a million letters. Reluctantly each time NBC agreed to continue Star Trek for another season. But they were

Spock, Kirk, and McCoy

never really happy about keeping it, and it was
given a new time slot: 10 o'clock on Friday
nights. That was a terrible time slot for a show
of this type, and after its third season Star Trek
was canceled because of "weak ratings"; no fan
interference could save it this time. Many connected with the show believed that NBC in-
tended to kill Star Trek no matter what happened. The final episode of the original Star
Trek series aired on June 3, 1969. The title of
the show was "Turnabout Intruder." The early

evening hour that was supposed to have gone to Star Trek was given to the comedy variety show "Laugh-In."

The real story of Star Trek popularity began after the series had been canceled. In the fall of 1969, the original seventy-nine episodes of Star Trek went into syndication. That is, they were sold to various independent local stations throughout the nation. These reruns proved to be enormously popular and became practically a permanent fixture on TV. The series always seems to be running somewhere in one's area. The reruns are scheduled for different hours, from late afternoon to late night. Anybody of any age can watch. A large percentage of Star Trek fans today weren't even born when the show went off the air. They grew up completely with Star Trek reruns.

When VCRs became widely available, fans began taping Star Trek episodes showing on their local TV stations. Now high-quality, commercially produced tapes of all of the original seventy-nine episodes are being produced and sold at video stores and through the mail. A complete library of Star Trek tapes should soon be available, thus ensuring that future generations of fans will continue to enjoy this remarkable TV series.

* * *

While no original Star Trek episodes were being produced, the series did inspire a series of cartoons, called Animateds by fans. The Animateds used the voices of William Shatner, Leonard Nimoy, and most of the other Star Trek regulars. Twenty-two Animateds were produced, and they originally ran between September 1973 and October 1974. Like the original live-action series, they have also been frequently rerun in syndication.

The adventures of the crew of the starship *Enterprise* have also appeared in book form. First there were "novelizations" of all of the TV episodes. That is, a novel was written from the original TV script. The novels, written by James Blish, followed the episode scripts exactly. These novels proved to be so popular that the series was expanded to include original novels, that is, stories about adventures of Kirk, Spock, and company that have never appeared on TV. There have also been comic books and records that have further expanded the adventures of the *Enterprise* and her crew.

With the continued popularity of Star Trek reruns, fans always hoped that the series would be revived, though it is very rare to revive a TV series once it has been canceled. Still, there were constant rumors that a new Star Trek series was planned. One of these rumors was

The animated Star Trek

true. In 1977 there was a plan to create a new TV network with a new version of Star Trek as one of the main attractions. Star Trek II was to cover the next five-year mission of the *Enterprise*. The crew was essentially to remain the same, with one major exception: Mr. Spock was no longer to be a regular, though it was hoped that he would often return as a guest star. His place as science officer was to be filled by Xon, a full-blooded Vulcan. Spock himself was to have returned to Vulcan to become head of the Science Academy, a post of great honor. Sets were built, costumes designed, and some scripts for Star Trek II were written, but not a single episode was ever filmed, because the plans for a fourth TV network fell through.

With a great deal of money already invested, the owners of Star Trek decided to make a movie instead. The result was *Star Trek: The Motion Picture,* which officially premiered at the MacArthur Theatre in Washington, D.C., on the evening of December 6, 1979.

Some of the changes that had originally been planned for the new Star Trek TV series were incorporated into the film. Among them were the addition of Commander Will Decker as first officer, and Lieutenant Ilia, a beautiful but bald native of Delta V, played in the film by Persis Khambatta.

Star Trek's loyal fans had speculated end--

lessly about the motion picture. Many feared that the old Star Trek magic would be lost in its move to the big screen. However, the transition was made with great care—it was the same Star Trek, except larger and more elaborate. A lot of critics thought that the film was too respectful, and rather overblown and boring. It had been terribly expensive to make, costing some $43 million. In contrast, the first Star Trek pilot had cost a mere $630,000. Shortly after the film came out it was widely referred to as a flop and a turkey. The death of Star Trek was predicted once again. And once again the critics and the cynics were wrong. The film earned some $170 million worldwide, and millions more from television. The videocassette of *Star Trek: The Motion Picture,* has become a best seller. Incidentally, the videocassette version restores fifteen minutes cut from the film as it was shown in theaters. Many believe that the restored scenes make the film much better. The ultimate success of *Star Trek: The Motion Picture* assured that there would be a *Star Trek II* (a film version), and that success assured a *Star Trek III* and a *Star Trek IV.* As the Trekkies have been saying for years now, STAR TREK LIVES!

Chapter 2

CAPTAIN KIRK

Though sometimes in danger of being over-whelmed by the very popular character of Mr. Spock, there was never any doubt in the minds of the creators of Star Trek, or in the minds of the actors who played the various characters, that James T. Kirk, Captain of the Starship *Enterprise* was the center of the entire Star Trek world. Most of the episodes of Star Trek revolve around Kirk's character and actions. The mandate of a Starfleet commander is a broad one, and with the *Enterprise* often out of communication with Starfleet bases for long periods of time, the captain was allowed great independence to make decisions that affected not only the welfare and very lives of his crew but the lives of a wide variety of alien races as well. Though bound by certain Federation rules, the captain of the *Enterprise* often encounters completely novel situations for which there are no rules. Kirk often shows a willingness to bend and even break rules when necessary. Captain Kirk feels his responsibilities very deeply. He is a truly heroic figure who makes good decisions more often than bad ones, but he is no superman, and according to Gene Roddenberry's original guide to Star Trek, he is "fully capable of letting the worry and frustration lead him into error."

When the series begins Kirk is in his mid-thirties, and holds the rank of captain with a starship command. Though little is told of his early life or family, we do know he was born in Iowa and that his ancestors were pioneers on the American frontier. Kirk has a deep interest in American history, and Abraham Lincoln is one of his heroes. Someone in his family must have had an interest in Roman history as well, for in one of the Animateds ("BEM," written by David Gerrold & D. C. Fontana) it is revealed that his middle initial stands for Tiberius. Just why James Kirk would have been named after the third Roman emperor, and a rather disreputable character, is unknown at present.

Kirk is a romantic, but he has considerable difficulty establishing any long-term relationship with a woman, though he is certainly attracted by women, and attractive to them. This mutual attraction exists no matter what planet or period in time Kirk finds himself. Often his attractiveness has been useful to him. In the "Gamesters of Triskelion," the drill-thrall Shahna falls for Kirk and spares his life in the arena. To be attracted to Kirk a female need not even be human, though generally they have assumed human form. The very alien witch Sylvia in "Catspaw" is not immune to his charm once she takes on a human shape, and in "By Any Other Name," Kelinda, a Kelvan who has taken human form, is both attracted and confused by Kirk's advances. But possibly Kirk's attraction was most fatal to the android Rayna in "Requiem for Methuselah." When forced to chose between Kirk, whom she has come to love, and Flint, her creator, her conflicts were so great that her circuits overloaded, and she was destroyed. Though the captain has sometimes been accused of using women, he is certainly no cold and thoughtless heartbreaker. In the case of Rayna, he was so affected that Spock had to use a mind touch to erase from his memory the unhappy incident. From time to time some of Kirk's old girlfriends reappear, like Areel Shaw, now a lawyer, who finds it difficult to prosecute Kirk in "Court Martial." There is also Dr. Janet Wallace, in "The Deadly

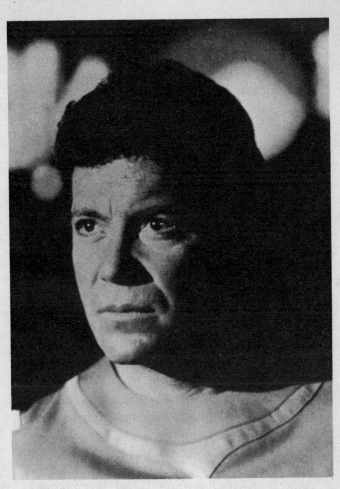

Kirk

Years," who parted from Kirk to pursue her own medical career, but turned up to help find a remedy for hyperaging radiation poisoning Kirk and others contracted on Gamma Hydra IV and save their lives. Then there is Ruth, from Kirk's Starfleet academy days. Jim Kirk remembers her fondly enough to materialize her image on the amusement park planet, and spend a pleasant shore leave with her in "Shore Leave."

Not all of Captain Kirk's past loves recall him fondly. In the final episode of the original Star Trek series, "Turnabout Intruder," Kirk meets up with another old flame, Janice Lester. At first Kirk does not realize that Janice, whom he once loved, has been driven insane by jealousy and ambition. She feels, unfairly, that Kirk walked out on her. She particularly hates Kirk's success in Starfleet and wants to become a starship commander. Janice manages to trap Kirk into a life-entity transfer in which she takes over his body, and he inhabits hers. After the transfer breaks, returning Janice to her own body, she still makes one last, unsuccessful attempt on the captain's life.

In *Star Trek II: The Wrath of Khan* we discover that Kirk has a son, David. His mother is the brilliant and beautiful Dr. Carol Marcus.

David is killed in *Star Trek III: The Search for Spock.*

Jim Kirk's brother, George Samuel "Sam" Kirk, a research biologist, and his wife Aurelan are killed in an attack of mass insanity spread by flying parasites in "Operation Annihilate!" Their son and Captain Kirk's nephew, Peter, a boy of about nine or ten, is the only survivor of the family.

Captain James T. Kirk's service record: Serial number SC937-0176CEC; Rank: captain with a starship command; Commendations: Palm Leaf of Axanar Peace Mission, Grankite Order of Tactics, Class of Excellence, Prantares Ribbon of Commendation, First and Second Class; Awards of valor: Medal of Honor, Silver Palm with Cluster, Starfleet Citation for Conspicuous Gallantry, Karagite Order of Heroism. By the time of *Star Trek: The Motion Picture* Kirk has become an admiral in Starfleet.

Kirk's leadership abilities have been fully recognized by Starfleet, and for that reason he was often chosen for difficult and sensitive missions. What is sometimes overlooked in all the praise that has been showered on Kirk for his bravery is his intelligence. As Spock has observed, when the captain is not overwhelmed by emotion he displays formidable powers of reasoning. He does, however, have more than a small measure of egotism, probably inevitable for a person who must bear such great responsibilities.

Despite this, Captain Kirk has never attempted to become anything more than an officer in Starfleet, though he has been tempted many times. In "Whom the Gods Destroy," Kirk is asked by Garth, once one of the finest military commanders in the galaxy and a hero of the young Starfleet cadet Jim Kirk, to help him take over the universe. Garth, of course, has gone completely mad. Kirk is saddened and taken aback by what has happened to his hero, but he is not moved to join the scheme of the self-styled "Master of the Universe." No other episode of Star Trek more clearly points up the difference between Kirk's well-developed, but thoroughly healthy ego and the power madness which can sometimes overtake the very talented.

Chapter 3

WILLIAM SHATNER

William Shatner is a Canadian, born in Montreal on March 22, 1931. Bill's father wanted him to come into the family clothing business, but he chose acting and joined Canada's National Repertory Theatre in Ottawa. The choice of profession was an odd one for young Bill, who had always regarded himself as a rather shy and withdrawn kid who disliked new places and meeting strangers. That is a doubly odd personality for the actor who would go on to play the captain of the starship that was to go "Where no man has gone before." There have been plenty of new places to go and strangers to meet in Star Trek.

Shatner first appeared on Broadway in a play called *Tamburlaine the Great* in 1956. He received some good reviews for his part in *The*

World of Susie Wong, which opened on Broadway in 1958. That same year he also got a part in the film *The Brothers Karamazov.* Shatner made one of his favorite films, *Judgement at Nuremberg,* in 1961.

He was no instant star. Like many other actors, Bill Shatner took what jobs he could get, appearing in summer stock, regional theater, and in a lot of television shows like "Twilight Zone" and "Outer Limits." At one point he appeared with another relatively unknown actor named Leonard Nimoy in an episode of the popular spy series, "The Man From U.N.C.L.E."

Though Star Trek has made Bill Shatner both rich and famous, he has remained a serious and committed actor. He can command a huge salary, but he will work for peanuts to do a role that he really likes. He has often worked with the Shakespeare festival in Stratford, Ontario. Shatner is also serious about his work in directing and scriptwriting.

Another of Bill Shatner's current enthusiasms is the horses that he rides and breeds on his southern California ranch.

One of the biggest problems that Shatner faced during the years of making the Star Trek TV series was his weight. Unlike Leonard

Nimoy, who is naturally thin, Shatner does tend to put on a few pounds. It's hard to hide extra poundage in a tight-fitting Starfleet uniform, and it was vital that Captain Kirk look trim and athletic. In his book *The World of Star Trek,* David Gerrold reports, "At one point, near the end of the second season, some very concerned memos were written about 'William Shatner's Equator.'" In some episodes directors tried to concentrate on close-ups so as not to show the star's expanding waistline. Shatner himself was well aware of the problem and would exercise vigorously in the time between seasons. But as shooting progressed and he became more fatigued (shooting a regular TV series is exhausting), he would begin to lose the energy to keep in shape. "Then I'd go on a crash diet—and I'd lose weight by the end of the season."

Shatner's long experience as an actor, writer, and director was very useful in making the Star Trek series. Though the basic themes of the series and characters had been set down in considerable detail by producer Gene Roddenberry, each episode had a different writer and different director, so the actors had a great deal of responsibility in maintaining the continuity of the series. Shatner would often make suggestions, and because he had so much experience, and because he was also the star of the show, he

Laughter was common on the Star Trek set.

was usually listened to. In Star Trek, William Shatner has done a lot more than act the part of Captain Kirk.

Shatner feels that one of the best things that he did with the Kirk character was develop his sense of humor. He found that during the first season Kirk seemed to be getting a bit stuffy and pompous. In order to avoid turning Captain Kirk into an overbearing bore, Shatner began to play him as a man who could laugh more easily at a situation and at himself. Shatner himself has an excellent sense of humor and was one of the bigger jokers on the Star Trek set.

For a while Shatner kept his dog, a giant black Doberman named Morgan, on the Star Trek set. The dog followed him everywhere, and while shooting was going on it was locked in his dressing room. No one walked into Bill Shatner's dressing room unless Bill was there; the dog saw to that.

Rumors of a great feud between Shatner and Nimoy circulated among Star Trek fans for years. It's a rumor that both men flatly deny. Everyone admits that there were occasional arguments and injured feelings not only between the two stars of the show but between all cast members. It's inevitable, given the pressures of producing a weekly, one-hour television show. Actors are together for ten to twelve hours a day, often under difficult and very stressful circumstances. Shatner points out that while Stark Trek was shooting he and Nimoy saw more of one another than they did of their wives. Frayed nerves, brought on by sheer fatigue, are a part of every television production. Both Shatner and Nimoy are actors who are proud of their work and of their performances, so there were bound to be differences of opinion, sometimes heated ones. But everyone connected with the show insists that the Star Trek cast was one of the happiest groups in television. Laughter was a lot more common than anger on the *Enterprise*.

Bill Shatner has not been content to rest on his Star Trek laurels and money. In recent years he appeared in the short-lived TV series "Barbary Coast," and had the title role in the more successful cop show "T. J. Hooker." He was also hilarious as a Kirk-like captain in the popular spoof film *Airplane II*.

Chapter 4

MR. SPOCK

Of all the Star Trek characters the most popular and most interesting is Mr. Spock, first officer and chief science officer aboard the *Enterprise*. Spock is an unusual hybrid, son of Sarek of Vulcan and Amanda Grayson of Terra. The children of such a marriage are apparently quite rare, for Spock has no brothers or sisters. Though he is half-human, in appearance he is a typical Vulcan and possesses most of the Vulcan characteristics, like copper-based blood and having "his heart where his liver should be," according to Dr. McCoy. Spock is also much stronger and more resistant to heat, radiation, and a variety of diseases than humans. Vulcans also have unique powers of telepathy.

Vulcan is a Class M planet, and home world for one of the Federation's most advanced and peaceful races. The Vulcans, however, have had a long and savage history; ultimately they came to reject their warlike past, and all the irrationality and emotionalism that can lead to violence. They have tried to breed or condition all irrationality out of themselves. As a result, Vulcan culture has led to a suppression of all emotions, and a cold, almost machinelike logic rules their lives. Sarek married Amanda Grayson because "It was the logical thing to do."

Spock has been raised as a Vulcan, and sometimes it seems as if he were trying to be more Vulcan than the full-blooded Vulcans. In the early episodes he acts as if he wishes to convince himself and others that he has no emotions at all. But though he tries to suppress all feeling, he is still half-human. It is the tension between these two sides of his personality that makes Spock such a fascinating character. A number of important Star Trek episodes turn on Spock's internal conflict. In many respects the Spock of the early Star Trek episodes is an unhappy, almost tragic figure. He is very much ashamed of his human heritage which he considers a weakness. Later he is able to relax and become more comfortable with his dual nature, but the essential conflict always remains.

When the series began, Spock was not a fully realized character, and certainly no one knew

An early version of the Spock makeup—

how popular he was to become. The character developed as Star Trek progressed. In the original Star Trek pilot film, later expanded into the two-part "The Menagerie," Spock looks and acts differently. His bangs are shorter and shaggier, his eyebrows thicker and even more upturned, and he seems less controlled, even smiling occasionally.

Spock's human emotions break through his Vulcan reserve on a number of occasions. In "The Naked Time," when a virus that relaxes inhibitions and brings out one's basic nature afflicts members of the *Enterprise* crew, Spock suddenly begins weeping over his mother. In "This Side of Paradise," it is spores that break down Spock's inhibitions, and he briefly falls in love with Leila Kalomi. He is also provoked into a fight with Kirk, but once the influence of the spores is neutralized Spock returns to his old unemotional self. Spock's most constant human emotion is his deepening friendship with Captain Kirk, which is one of the main underlying themes of both the TV series and the films.

While Vulcans are supposed to be logical, the relationship between Spock and his fully Vulcan father has a curiously illogical side. When as a young man Spock chose to enter Starfleet rather than enter the Vulcan Academy of Sciences, Sarek was so angered he refused to speak to his son for eighteen years. Spock reveres his father, but is equally stubborn about making up. They must be lectured by the very human Amanda before a reconciliation can be brought about. In the film *Star Trek III: The Search for Spock* Sarek is deeply concerned over the apparent fate of his only son.

It isn't just the human side of his nature that causes Spock emotional problems; his purely Vulcan side also contains dangerous elements. In "All Our Yesterdays," Spock is sent into the past, and reverts to the prelogical behavior of the Vulcans, nearly killing McCoy in a jealous rage. But the fullest exploration of the theme of past Vulcan savagery comes in the episode "Amok Time," when Spock is consumed by the Vulcan mating urge—*pon farr* in the Vulcan language; he becomes irrational, ill, and almost mad. He is taken back to Vulcan to claim T'Pring, whom he had been betrothed to in childhood. But she doesn't want him anymore, and he must fight to the death in order to claim her. That is another ancient Vulcan custom, from the old, savage, prelogical days. T'Pring chooses Kirk as her champion, and in the struggle Spock kills Kirk, or at least believes he does. This killing comes as such a shock that it suppresses Spock's mating urge; he surrenders T'Pring and goes back to the *Enterprise*. He then discovers that Kirk is not really dead and momentarily gives way to another emotion—great joy—before returning to his usual logical and unemotional Vulcan ways. The Vulcan *pon farr* comes up again in *Star Trek III*, when Spock goes through accelerated growth on the Genesis planet.

For a race as unemotional and private as the Vulcans, telepathy can be something of an embarrassment, but they do possess telepathic powers in various degrees. At moments of extreme crisis Vulcans can become mentally aware of one another over vast distances. In "The Immunity Syndrome," Spock receives a severe mental jolt when the starship *Intrepid*, manned by four hundred Vulcans, is destroyed, though it is light-years away from the *Enterprise*. Generally the Vulcan telepathy operates only when the two subjects are actually touching. This telepathic ability extends beyond reading the minds of other Vulcans or humans to reading the thoughts of totally alien life forms, even of nonliving things. Spock uses the Vulcan mind-touch to read the thoughts of the vast cosmic cloud, really an utterly alien living being from another galaxy. He also reads the "mind" of the mad satellite Nomad, in "The Changeling," through the use of the Vulcan mind-touch. In *Star Trek: The Motion Picture*, Spock completes a mind-meld with the "living machine" V'ger. Spock uses his extraordinary mental powers to remove Kirk's memory of an unhappy love in "Requiem for Methuselah," and to restore Kirk's memory in "The Paradise Syndrome." He is also able to transfer his own personality to the mind of Dr. McCoy when his body is apparently doomed at the end of *Star Trek II,* and the personality is transferred back into Spock's restored body during *Star Trek III.* The telepathic powers of the Vulcans are indeed formidable.

In the highly technological Star Trek world, the apparently simple Vulcan nerve pinch or Vulcan neck pinch has proved to be an unusually effective weapon for Spock. With it he can render a person immediately unconscious by a pinch on the neck or shoulder. Because the Vulcans have great strength and a detailed knowledge of anatomy, only they seem able to master the simple-looking technique. Spock has tried to teach it to Captain Kirk, but without success. The Vulcan nerve pinch should not be confused with the "Vulcan death grip," which is supposed to be lethal pressure applied to the face and forehead. However, there is no "death grip." Spock uses it as a ruse to fool the Romulans.

The Vulcan salute is made with the right hand, palm facing the person you are greeting, fingers spread in the middle. A much more intimate greeting is the Vulcan ritual embrace,

The Vulcan salute

where hands are crossed at the wrist with palms touching the other's palms. This greeting is suitable only for members of one's family.

The Vulcan sun is so bright that Vulcans have evolved an extra eyelid to protect their eyes

30

from the light. This extra eyelid saves Spock's sight when, in "Operation: Annihilate!" he is subjected to fierce light to rid him of a dangerous parasite.

In addition to having immense scientific knowledge, Spock is also highly cultured, with a keen appreciation of Terran art. In "Requiem for Methuselah," he is able to recognize da Vinci's painting technique and Brahm's signature. He even expresses envy of Flint's collection of art, a rare expression of human emotion. Spock can sight-read music and can play the musical instrument the Vulcan lyre. Nor has Spock ignored Terran literature. He has quoted Shakespeare, Byron, Blake, and Poe, and has several times quoted from the Bible.

Though Spock has been an officer with Starfleet for many years, he shows no ambition to become a starship commander. Even when thrown into an alternate universe ruled by treachery and force in "Mirror Mirror," Spock's counterpart, known as Spock 2, remains remarkably civilized when compared with a murderous Kirk 2. Spock 2 also shows great reluctance to take over the mirror universe's counterpart of the *Enterprise*. He is the only one in the bloodthirsty crew who is not plotting to take over the ship.

Chapter 5

LEONARD NIMOY

A great deal of the success of the Spock character is rightly attributed to the actor who plays the part, Leonard Nimoy. Nimoy was born on March 26, 1931, graduated from Southern California University, and received most of his early acting training at the Pasadena Playhouse in California. Before Star Trek his career had not been a spectacular one. He had appeared briefly in a number of TV shows like "Dragnet," "Thriller," "Outer Limits," and "The Lieutenant." He had even appeared in what has been described as an "incredibly bad" B science fiction film, *The Brain Eaters*. David Gerrold has written, "Fortunately, it was a very small part and he was heavily made up. If you didn't know it was Leonard, you'd never recognize him."

Gene Roddenberry was executive producer of "The Lieutenant" when Nimoy appeared in one of the episodes. Roddenberry liked what he saw and contacted Nimoy's agent about the pilot for Star Trek. Nimoy was flattered, but he didn't get too excited at first because he knew it was a long trip between writing a pilot and actually getting a show on the air. Most pilots never make it.

At first the only well-established features of the Spock character were that he was half-human, half-alien and that he had pointy ears. It was the ears that gave Nimoy the most trouble. The first pair of ears he got were, in Nimoy's word's, "gruesome." A new makeup man supplied a more delicate, natural-looking "appliance"—that's the term used by makeup artists for such things as false ears and false noses. Still, the ears could be painful to wear. "They irritated, particularly inside the ear when they had to be glued down." Each appliance lasted only a few days, and each felt a little different. But Nimoy got used to them. "They say you can get used to hanging by your thumbs," he commented.

No definite decision had been made about Spock's skin color. He started out with reddish skin, which was fine for color TV, but back in the 60's a lot of people still had black-and-white sets, and in black and white the reddish skin made Nimoy look like he was wearing a lot of phony makeup. So the skin color was changed to yellowish, which looked better in black and white. It was reasoned that a Vulcan's skin was yellow because his blood was copper-based. Some local stations have tried to remedy this by adjusting the color to give Spock a greenish hue.

Nimoy didn't have a great deal to do in filming the first pilot. It took about three weeks, which he admits was the longest acting job he had ever had up to that time. "So this one was a giant project—very esoteric show, very cerebral. It scared everybody half to death because it cost a fortune and most of the network people didn't understand it." After filming the pilot, Nimoy figured that was the end of that, and almost forgot about Star Trek until he was asked back to do a second pilot. And then the show went on the air.

The success of Star Trek and the intensity of fan loyalty came as a surprise to all of those who had been involved in creating the show. The fan response to the character of Spock was more than a surprise—it was a complete shock. At first Nimoy tried to answer all his fan mail personally by hand. The first week the show was on the air he got thirty-five letters. Within a month he was getting sacks of mail every day.

When he made personal appearances the crowds were sometimes so large and enthusiastic that the police had trouble holding them back. Some places wouldn't even let him appear because they felt they couldn't handle the crowds.

Nimoy invented the Vulcan salute. He said that he got the idea from a blessing used by rabbis. The gesture was first used in the episode "Amok Time." Not everyone can split their fingers the proper way, and Nimoy said that it was fortunate that actress Celia Lovsky, who played the Vulcan Matriarch, T'Pau, could do it, otherwise the gesture probably would have been abandoned before it was ever shown on the air.

Many of the other Vulcan characteristics developed as the show went along. In one episode Spock was supposed to come up behind a temporarily deranged Kirk and hit him with the butt of his phaser, but Nimoy didn't like the idea. He said it sounded like a hangover from Westerns. So he invented the Vulcan nerve pinch. Roddenberry came up with the Vulcan mind-meld in the episode "Dagger of the Mind" because a scene where Spock was supposed to be questioning someone wasn't working. Spock had to get more deeply into the man's past, so he was made telepathic.

Of all those who have appeared on Star Trek, Nimoy has been most closely associated with the character he plays. Sometimes the association has been too close, for his autobiography was entitled *I Am Not Spock.*

Nimoy's career outside Star Trek has included a regular role on the series "Mission Impossible," and host/narrator of the series "In Search of . . ." and "Lights, Camera, Action." He has appeared on Broadway in the play *Equus* and toured with the one-man show *Vincent,* based on the life of the painter Vincent van Gogh. He has also recorded many albums, among them "The Way I Feel" and "Mr. Spock's Music From Outer Space."

Throughout the shooting of *Star Trek II,* it was generally assumed that the film would be Nimoy's last outing as Spock. Spock was to die at the end of the film and that would be that. Fans picked up rumors of this and were nearly hysterical. Somewhere along the line Nimoy decided that he wanted to continue to do the character. Director Nicholas Meyer added some shots showing Spock's coffin, which indicated that while Spock was dead, he might not be *permanently* dead. He had, after all, survived apparent permanent death in several of the Star Trek television episodes.

When Nimoy first appeared in the Star Trek

Spock

pilot he had been studying directing, but he never got a chance to direct a film until *Star Trek III*, a multimillion-dollar project. Not only was he to appear in the film he was also to direct it. Though there had been some feeling among the cast that having one of the stars as director of the film might create serious problems on the set, practically everybody connected with *Star Trek III* said that it went smoothly and pleasantly, and was the easiest of the Star Trek movies to make. Nimoy also directs the latest Star Trek film, *Star Trek IV: The Voyage Home*.

Chapter 6

THE CREW

Lieutenant Commander Leonard McCoy, the senior ship surgeon and head of the medical department of the *Enterprise,* is a man of about forty-five when the series begins. He is a curious mixture of cynicism and sentiment. On the surface he is extremely sarcastic, often making biting comments about others. Beneath the surface, and not very far beneath, he is a man of deep feelings. He is also basically a gallant Southern gentleman of the old school. He was born in Georgia, and during moments of excitement his accent can be detected. McCoy is a mass of contradictions. He is head of a highly advanced medical team and has an impressive scientific background, yet he is at heart an old-fashioned country doctor. Kirk calls him "Bones," a short version of "Sawbones," an old term for a doctor. McCoy really dislikes and distrusts much of the advanced technology that he uses. For example, in early episodes of the Star Trek series McCoy expresses his discomfort with using the transporter.

A key conflict in Star Trek is the running feud between McCoy, feeling, emotional, and profoundly illogical, and the very logical, outwardly unfeeling Spock. While McCoy is often illogical and occasionally even irrational and professes to despise cold logic, he recognizes, as Spock does not, that people often are illogical and ruled by their emotions. McCoy regards Spock as irritating and smug, but he also recognizes that Spock is tormented by his dual nature. While many Star Trek episodes end with the pair exchanging sharp comments, it is also clear that they have deep respect for one another.

McCoy was once married, but is divorced. It's a part of his life he doesn't talk about. He has a daughter Joanna who is training to be a nurse. Like many other members of the *Enterprise* crew, McCoy is from time to time con-

McCoy

fronted with figures from his past. In the very first Star Trek episode broadcast, "The Man Trap," McCoy meets one of his old girlfriends, Nancy Crater. Kirk and Spock have a difficult time convincing the romantic doctor that what he takes to be Nancy is really a salt vampire, a creature that has the power of creating the illusion that it is a human being.

When the crew of the *Enterprise* again gathers after ten years in *Star Trek: The Motion Picture,* they seem to have changed remarkably little, all except McCoy, who appears with a bushy brown beard. He soon shaves it.

DeForest Kelley, who plays Dr. McCoy, was not one of the original cast members of Star Trek. He had first been scheduled to do another Gene Roddenberry pilot, "Police Story." That pilot never sold, but Kelley's performance rated high with a preview audience. By that time the second Star Trek pilot had already been shot, and the show was ready to go on the air. Roddenberry then asked Kelley to take the part of the doctor. That second pilot, "Where No Man Has Gone Before," was the third program to be aired, and it is one of the few in which McCoy does not appear. The first pilot was re-edited with new scenes, and broadcast as the two-part show "The Menagerie." The McCoy character is included in those extra scenes. The first doctor on the *Enterprise* was played by John Hoyt, the second by Paul Fix.

Lieutenant Commander Montgomery Scott, or "Scotty," the chief engineer on the *Enterprise,* is really more of a tinkerer than a high-tech type. There are times that he seems to be holding the great starship together with little more than spit and baling wire.

Scotty feigns a distrust of women, but he is in fact very fond of them. In the episode "Who Mourns for Adonais?" Scotty is very much taken with Lieutenant Carolyn Palamas and is heartbroken when she deserts him for the Greek god Apollo. In "The Lights of Zetar," he falls deeply in love with Lieutenant Mira Romaine. In "Wolf in the Fold," he becomes infatuated with a nightclub dancer and is later accused of her brutal murder. At first McCoy wonders if Scott's subconscious distrust of women has not been turned homicidal by a serious head injury. As it turns out, Scott wasn't responsible for the murder at all.

Of the many phrases made popular by Star Trek, the most familiar is "Beam me up, Scotty." Variations of this phrase have often been found on bumper stickers. One reads

"Beam me up, Scotty, there's no intelligent life on this planet."

James Doohan, who plays Scott, was a hard-working and successful actor in Canada before Star Trek. A lot of his success was due to his ability to do a large number of different voices and accents, and he had worked extensively on radio. When he was called in to read for the part of the engineer in Star Trek, Roddenberry apparently did not have a clear idea of what the character was supposed to sound like. Doohan was asked to do Russian, German, Irish, English, and Scottish accents. Roddenberry and his associates liked the Scottish accent best. In one episode, "Return to Tomorrow," Doohan not only played Scotty but was the voice of the alien Saragon as well.

In an episode where Scotty wears a kilt as part of his dress uniform, he is actually wearing the tartan design of the Scott clan, one of the oldest of the Scottish tartans.

Scotty is known for his appreciation of fine drink and has a collection of alcoholic beverages from all known parts of the galaxy. Occasionally his fondness for drink has come in very handy indeed, as in "By Any Other Name," when he is able, after heroic efforts, to get one of the Kelvans who have invaded the *Enterprise* drunk.

According to Doohan, Scott was first sup-

Scotty

Sulu

posed to be a very minor character. He had just a few lines to say in the pilot, and in the beginning he was contracted to do only four or five of the first thirteen episodes. But the character proved to be too useful. When Spock and Kirk were beamed down to some planet, the chief engineer was the logical choice to take care of the ship. Besides, Doohan's character proved very appealing to Star Trek viewers.

Lieutenant Sulu is the chief helmsman aboard the *Enterprise*. He's extremely efficient. The captain never has to give him an order twice. He's also an enthusiastic botanist, a collector of antique firearms, and an expert fencer, a skill that he gets to show off in "The Naked Time," when a virus loosens his inhibitions and he runs wild with a fencing foil.

George Takei, who plays Sulu, was not in the initial Star Trek pilot, but he was in the second pilot and in most of the episodes of the series, as well as in the films. For the first season, however, he had very little to do. "I used to have my lines memorized even before I saw the script. 'Aye, aye, sir,' 'Coming to new course,' and 'Phasers locked on target.'" He missed filming a number of episodes during the second season because he was doing the film *The Green Berets* with John Wayne. Even in a small part Takei was able to establish a presence that has made him one of the most recognizable of the regular Star Trek cast.

Lieutenant Uhura is a native of the United States of Africa. Her name means "freedom" in the Swahili language. On duty she is the highly efficient communications officer of the *Enterprise*. Off duty she is the most musical member of the regular crew. She sings in several episodes, and very well, too.

The episode "Plato's Stepchildren," first aired on November 22, 1968, is famous in television history because in it Kirk and Uhura kiss. This is the first interracial kiss ever shown on a nationally televised series.

Nichelle Nichols, who plays Uhura, had done work on the stage but got her first television role in Roddenberry's "The Lieutenant." When that show was winding down, Roddenberry asked her to read for a part in his new series Star Trek. She was the last regular member of the cast to be chosen before the show went on the air and did not appear in either of the pilot episodes. However, she is the only female member of the cast of Star Trek to have appeared in all three television seasons and in all of the Star Trek films.

Ensign Pavel Andreievich Chekov joined the crew of the *Enterprise* as navigator following

Uhura

Chekov

the death of Lieutenant Commander Gary Mitchell, in "Where No Man Has Gone Before," and a series of temporary replacements. The young, charming, and impressionable Russian quickly became one of the most popular regular members of the *Enterprise* crew.

Walter Koenig, who plays Chekov, didn't join Star Trek until the second season, and at first he was hired only on a show-to-show basis. Audience reaction to him was so favorable that by the third season he was given a regular contract. His big break came during the second season when George Takei (Sulu) had to take about ten weeks off to film *The Green Berets.* Many of the things that Sulu was supposed to do were then given to Chekov, which increased the size of his part significantly. In later episodes, like "Spectre of the Gun," he had very nearly a starring role, and he got good parts in the films as well.

By *Star Trek II,* Chekov has left the *Enterprise* to become first officer on the *Reliant,* a major promotion in Starfleet, but he happily rejoins his old companions at the film's end.

Nurse Christine Chapel first appears prominently in the episode "What Are Little Girls Made Of?". The *Enterprise* is searching for her fiancé Dr. Roger Korby. After Korby's death she stays on the *Enterprise* as McCoy's aid, and soon falls hopelessly in love with Spock. She first confesses her love to Spock in "The Naked Time," and continues to pursue him without any success or encouragement. Nurse Chapel's attentions only make Spock vaguely uncomfortable and he tries to avoid her as much as possible, though he does show occasional moments of tenderness.

Of all the series regulars the character of Christine Chapel seems to have been the least popular with fans. It appears that some have resented her pursuit of Spock.

Nurse Chapel was played by actress Majel Barrett, who in 1969 married series producer Gene Roddenberry. She also supplied the voice of the *Enterprise*'s all-knowing computer.

Yeoman Janice Rand figures prominently in some of the early Star Trek episodes. She and Kirk appear to like one another. But after a while she realizes that Kirk is married to his ship, so she transfers out. But Janice Rand comes back again briefly for the grand reunion of *Star Trek: The Motion Picture*. She is also in *Star Trek III* and *IV*.

Other members of the *Enterprise* crew who popped up from time to time were navigator Lieutenant Kevin Riley, who is memorable for his repeated, off-key rendition of the Irish song "I'll Take You Home Again, Kathleen" in "The Naked Time," and Dr. M'Benga, an African doctor who is a specialist in Vulcan medicine, having interned in a Vulcan hospital.

Chapter 7

THE *ENTERPRISE*

The U.S.S. *Enterprise* is one of twelve starships of the Constellation class. When the Star Trek series began she was regarded as the most modern type of vessel in Starfleet. But time catches up with the gallant vessel. By *Star Trek: The Motion Picture* the *Enterprise* needs extensive refitting, though in the scene where she moves majestically out of her orbiting drydock she looks better than she ever has. But by *Star Trek III* the *Enterprise* is clearly becoming an obsolete vessel, inferior in range and equipment to a newer vessel like the *Excelsior*.

In its original conception, Star Trek was the "voyages of the starship *Enterprise*." The vessel itself was to be central to the show. As the series progressed, the characters, particularly Kirk and Spock, became the real focus. But the

Enterprise was always there, a unifying force for the series. The first sight of the *Enterprise* in *Star Trek: The Motion Picture* is still the finest scene in the film, and one that brings tears to the eyes of devoted Trekkies. Throughout the series this gallant ship has been shot at with a variety of beams and other weapons and nearly destroyed in an amazing number of different ways. She has been crippled in battle and blasted through time itself. Yet she always seemed to survive. But at the end of *Star Trek III*, the *Enterprise* appears to have been completely destroyed, an event that has caused great consternation among the fans. She may be gone, but she will never be forgotten.

In her heyday the *Enterprise* had a crew of 430—mostly human. The prominent "saucer section" had eleven decks with the bridge— scene of much of the action of Star Trek—at the top. The large, cylinderlike and highly complex engineering section is located beneath the main section. Two additional cylindrical sections, called nacelles, are attached to the engineering section. All parts of the ship are connected by a system of highly efficient turbolifts.

The bridge is the heart and brain of the *Enterprise*. At the center of the bridge is the captain's command chair. In front of the captain sit the navigator and the helmsmen at their consoles, all facing a large viewscreen. In the outer

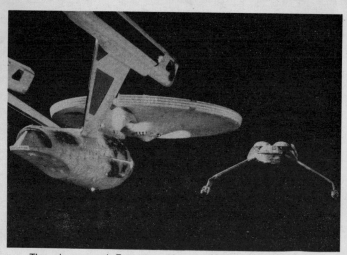

The damaged *Enterprise* faces a Klingon ship in *Star Trek III.*

circle of the bridge sit the communications officer and various other technical officers. The science officer has his own console known as the library/computer station. The science officer also oversees the sensors used to detect activity outside of the ship.

While the bridge is in many respects the "brain" of the *Enterprise,* a second brain is surely the computer which is located deep within the vessel, but is able to communicate by voice with the bridge and all other parts of the ship. The computer sets the course and automatically maintains the life-support systems, including atmosphere and gravity. (If the computer somehow fails, individual functions can be switched to manual override.) In addition to running many of the purely mechanical functions of the ship, the computer also has stored within its vast memory practically the entire accumulated knowledge of the human and several other races. Much of the communication with the computer is done through bridge console, but it can also be connected to stations and viewscreens throughout the ship.

While the *Enterprise* computer—it has no name—is supposed to be nothing more than a supremely efficient machine, a personality of sorts has emerged. The computer speaks in a mechanical voice that, while it is supposed to be neutral, tends to sound intolerant and a bit priggish when someone makes a mistake or enters ambiguous data. In one episode, "Tomorrow Is Yesterday," the computer has just undergone repairs on a female-dominated planet and has picked up a female voice and a few idiosyncracies; for example, it insists on calling Kirk "dear." Though most of the work done by computer on the *Enterprise* is quite serious, it can, when necessary, do more mundane tasks. In "And the Children Shall Lead," the computer's food synthesizer serves up ice-cream sundaes to a group of children.

* * *

The galaxy is unimaginably vast. Even traveling at the speed of light the voyages of the *Enterprise* would take hundreds of years, so the starship needs a power that will allow it to exceed the speed of light to reach hyperlight speeds. This is warp drive, a power which allows the starship literally to bend or warp space. In order to generate the power for warp drive, the *Enterprise* engines use integrated matter and antimatter. The annihilation of matter and antimatter creates the necessary power. Dilithium crystals are used to channel the warp drive power. This power system can be dangerous if the matter/antimatter shielding breaks down. The starship is constructed so that the nacelles containing the power source can be blown away from the rest of the ship in an emergency.

The hyperlight speed of the *Enterprise* is measured in warp factors—warp factor 1 is the speed of light, 186,000 miles per second. As the warp factors go up, the speed increases geometrically—warp 2 is eight times the speed of light, warp 3 is twenty-seven times the speed of light, warp 4 is sixty-four times the speed of light, etc. Above warp 6, warp speeds become dangerous, and the *Enterprise* will go to warp 7 or 8 only in extreme emergencies. At warp 8 the ship shows considerable strain; at warp 9 even time becomes distorted, and the *Enterprise*'s instruments are no longer reliable.

When operating at sublight speed, the *Enterprise* uses impulse power generated at the rear of the "saucer section." Impulse power is based on the same principles as rocket power.

We are given a good view of the bridge of the *Enterprise*, which is very well designed, and we occasionally see the captain's cabin or those of some of the other officers, but we know virtually nothing of the accommodations of the 400 odd other crew members. Did they sleep in barracks or do all have their own staterooms? Roddenberry himself favored the idea of separate staterooms for the crew. He felt that Starfleet would not treat its enlistees like cattle, as the military often does today. However, the Star Trek producers never had the luxury of building a full-scale model of the *Enterprise*—it would have been a monumental, multimillion-dollar task, anyway. If a set didn't figure directly into a story then it just wasn't built, and the complete crew quarters never figured directly in a story. We do, however, get glimpses of several individual crewmen's quarters.

The main defense for the *Enterprise* or any other starship is its deflectors, an invisible force barrier which will protect the ship from most known weapons. The deflectors are activated automatically when the ship is under attack. However, they are a tremendous drain on power, and maximum shielding can be maintained for only about twenty hours. The transporter room, which also draws a great deal of power, cannot be used while the deflector screen is operating.

While deflectors keep objects away from the *Enterprise,* the tractor beam has just the opposite effect: its purpose is to pull things toward the ship. It is used to tow a smaller ship or help the *Enterprise* maintain a stable position alongside a larger one. The tractor beam, which has a range of about 100,000 miles, has also been used to pull objects within the range of the transporter, which can operate only within a much more limited area.

The uniforms worn by members of the *Enterprise* crew have changed somewhat over the years. For most of the series the standard men's uniform was a shirt, whose color indicated the crewmen's department, and black, flare-bottom pants with black boots. The women wore a short skirt, with matching panties and boots. Shirt colors were golden yellow for command, blue for sciences, and red for engineering and most other jobs. There were also some full-dress uniforms worn occasionally. A small patch or insignia worn on the left side of the uniform shirt indicated which ship an individual came from. For the *Enterprise* the symbol was a stylized arrowhead. In the films the uniforms tended to be jackets and tunics rather than shirts. There was more decoration, and the arrowhead insignia became even more stylized.

One of the things that makes the position of starship captain so responsible and difficult is that he is often out of touch with his superiors at Starfleet command. The starship's main means of communication with its bases is through the use of subspace radio, which utilizes a space warp effect to carry messages at speeds far exceeding that of the ship itself. But even with this means of communication the starship captain often finds it very difficult to contact a starbase for additional instructions or information. Most of the time he is on his own.

For short trips (relatively speaking), the crew of the *Enterprise* can use a six- or seven-passenger shuttlecraft. The *Enterprise* had at least two of these craft, the *Columbus* and the *Galileo,* which was destroyed after an accident-filled career.

The primary means of moving from the *Enterprise* to the surface of a planet is the trans-

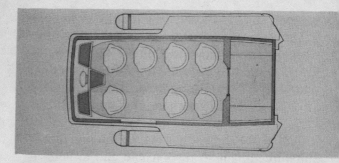

Shuttlecraft from the *Enterprise*

porter. The transporter temporarily converts matter into energy, beams the energy to a fixed point, and then reassembles the matter in its original form. The range of the transporter is about 16,000 miles. The distance is covered almost instantaneously, but it is possible to suspend an individual in transit. The transporter draws a tremendous amount of energy and is very risky to use when the ship's power is low. Generally the transporter works without a hitch, but McCoy has voiced some suspicion of the device, claiming that the instant of dematerialization is a form of nonexistence. No one else on the *Enterprise* seems particularly worried about this.

There are a number of transporter rooms aboard the *Enterprise*. The main transporter room, with a console usually operated by Scotty, can handle up to six people at a time.

The artificial gravity aboard the *Enterprise* works remarkably well. Even when the ship is severely disabled, which it has been on many occasions, this system practically never fails.

When faced with an extreme emergency—the inevitable capture of the *Enterprise* by hostile forces—the ship can be destroyed by activating the destruct sequence from the bridge. It must be done in the following manner:

Kirk: "Computer, this is Captain James Kirk of the U.S.S. *Enterprise*. Destruct sequence one, code one, one-A." The computer then repeats the information.

Spock: "This is Commander Spock, science officer. Destruct sequence two, code one, one-

A, two-B." Again the computer repeats the information.

Scott: "This is Lieutenant Commander Scott, chief engineering officer of the U.S.S. *Enterprise*. Destruct sequence number three, code one-B, two-B, three."

Computer: "Destruct sequence completed and engaged; awaiting code for thirty-second countdown."

Kirk: "Code zero, zero, zero, destruct zero."

Computer: "Thirty seconds, twenty-nine, twenty-eight, twenty-seven . . ."

The deadly countdown can be stopped up to five seconds before destruction if Kirk gives the computer this code:

"Code one, two, three continuity: abort destruct order."

If the destruct sequence passes the five-second mark, then there is no command in the galaxy that can stop it.

The original model of the starship *Enterprise* is in the Smithsonian Institute along with models of the Wright brothers' airplane, Charles Lindbergh's *Spirit of St. Louis,* and the Apollo astronauts' craft.

Chapter 8

STAR TREK TECHNOLOGY

Though the mission of the *Enterprise* is an entirely peaceful one, hostile forces have been encountered, so weapons are sometimes necessary. The primary weapon is the phaser. It's a beam that can be set either to stun or to kill. At its lowest power it will simply quiet someone; at a slightly higher power it can knock out a man, or most other species, without producing any lasting ill effects; at still higher powers the phaser can cause an object to explode, burn, or completely dematerialize. The phaser can also be used as a bomb. When set on overload it will explode, destroying everything around it. In addition to being used as a weapon it can be used as a tool, like a cutting torch, or for heating rocks in order to provide warmth. The higher the power the more visible the phaser beam becomes.

Phasers come in two sizes. The smallest is the hand-held phaser, which fits easily into the palm of the hand. That is the weapon normally used by landing parties from the *Enterprise* when a larger phaser would look too obvious or aggressive. The hand-held phaser is carried in the belt along with the communicator—both are about the same size. The phaser pistol is larger and more powerful and is also carried on the belt, but it is clearly displayed as a weapon. The most powerful phasers are those mounted aboard the *Enterprise* itself. They are the ship's primary weapons. The phasers are on the saucer section of the ship and are generally controlled by Sulu under Kirk's direction.

In addition to its banks of phasers, the *Enterprise* is also equipped with photon torpedoes. These were originally developed by the Romulans and proved so effective that they were copied by scientists of the Federation. The photon torpedoes employ a pod of matter/ antimatter which can track a target at a speed of many warp factors. The torpedo has a limited lifespan, so a ship can outrun one until it disappears, but it isn't easy.

One of the most important devices used by any *Enterprise* landing party is the communicator. This hand-held device attaches to the belt and is activated by flipping open the antenna. It is used mainly by members of a landing party to communicate with one another and with the *Enterprise*. The communicator has the same 16,000-mile range as the transporter. One of the most important, and most frequent messages spoken over the communicator is "Beam me up." Communicators are rarely used aboard the *Enterprise*, where there are other means of communication.

The tricorder is a remarkably versatile miniaturized device that can be used to sense, analyze, identify, and keep records on practically anything an *Enterprise* landing party might encounter. The tricorder is easily portable, about the size of a book, and is carried with a shoulder strap, often by Spock and McCoy. It can detect the presence of alien life (life-form readings) or give the age of an artifact. The range of the tricorder is about one hundred miles. Dr. McCoy has a special medical tricorder to help him in diagnosis.

Though McCoy cannot truly resurrect the dead, he does have at his command instruments that are effective in restarting stopped human (or Vulcan) hearts and in steadying the heartbeat. These devices are called the physiostimulator and the cardiostimulator. The differences between the two are unclear.

Most of the planets visited by the *Enterprise*

have atmospheres that are not hostile to human or Vulcan life, so elaborate protective clothing is rarely needed. But for the vacuum of space, a type of space suit, called an environmental suit, is used.

A number of Star Trek episodes involve time travel. For example, on Sarpeidon there is the atavachron, which can send the Sarpeids back into their own past. Anyone who intends to use the atavachron must have his brain and body properly prepared or he will be unable to adjust to the era into which he is sent. An unprepared individual will die within a few hours. In "All Our Yesterdays," Kirk, Spock, and McCoy are accidentally thrown back into the past by the atavachron.

The power-crazed Dr. Tristan Adams, director of the penal colony Tantalus V, invented the neural neutralizer, a brainwashing device, in "Dagger of the Mind." The exact workings of the neural neutralizer are unknown, for it was dismantled. When in operation the subject would sit in a chair and be subjected to a beam.

There are a variety of force fields in use throughout the galaxy. These transparent, impenetrable shields are used either to keep something in, like prisoners, or keep something out, like intruders. Sometimes, as in "Spectre of the Gun," the force field of the Melkots is so powerful that it prevents ordinary instruments like phasers and communicators from operating. It is probable that there are many different types of force fields, since they are employed by so many races in the galaxy and beyond. Some are generated by machine, others by mental or psychic powers, and a few seem to be the result of pure magic.

The Romulans have developed an invisibility screen called a cloaking device, which hides a ship from observations and from most scanners. However, the system has its drawbacks. A major drawback is that those inside the cloaking device cannot see out, and therefore a ship must become visible in order to fight.

Not all of the devices used in Star Trek are high tech. There is, for example, an ancient Vulcan weapon, the *ahn-woon*—a leather thong with handles at each end that can be used as a sling or a garrote. In "Amok Time," Spock strangles Kirk with an *ahn-woon*.

Chapter 9

VILLAINS

The Khan of *Star Trek II: The Wrath of Khan* is Khan Noonian Singh, who from 1992 to 1996 was absolute ruler of one-quarter of the Earth, from South Asia to the Middle East. Khan was one of a group of selectively bred "supermen" who took over the Earth in the 1990s. They were defeated when the "normals" revolted in what was called the Eugenics Wars. Khan was the last of the tyrants to be driven from power, but he escaped in the "sleeper ship" *Botany Bay* with eighty of his people. A "sleeper ship" is a prewarp-drive ship in which the crew is placed in suspended animation. More than two hundred years later Khan's ship was found by the *Enterprise* in the episode "Space Seed." Khan has not changed one bit during his long sleep. He tries to take over the *Enterprise* so he can be transported back to civilization and

Khan

once again resume his career of conquest.
Khan manages to captivate the *Enterprise*'s
historian, Lieutenant Marla McGivers, but this
"superman" ultimately cannot outsmart or out-
fight the combination of Kirk and Spock. He is
defeated, and with his followers and Lieutenant
McGivers, is sent into exile on Ceti Alpha V.

In *Star Trek II*, Khan returns, older, shaggier, and meaner than ever. Marla has died hor-
ribly on Ceti, and Khan blames Kirk for all his
troubles. Indeed, he has become insanely ob-
sessed with getting even with Kirk.

Portraying Khan, both in the TV show and
the movie, was veteran actor Ricardo Montalban, who was superb, particularly in the

film. He was the classic villain. Montalban, who has had a long movie career, was already familiar to TV audiences in much more benign roles, as a salesman for luxury cars in a long series of ads, and as the host of the series "Fantasy Island."

In the episode "The Squire of Gothos," the *Enterprise* meets a figure named Trelane on the planet Gothos. Trelane is, in many respects, the ultimate spoiled brat. He is the child of a race of noncorporeal beings with tremendous powers, though he appears to be a rather handsome middle-aged man. Trelane is in love with Earth history, particularly the eighteenth century and the military. He is not truly evil, but he is totally self-centered, lacking in control, and possesses a streak of cruelty. Given his great powers he is a dangerous adversary. Outwardly Trelane is charming and cultured, but if thwarted in any way he can turn murderous, and he very nearly kills Kirk. Then Trelane's parents, seen only as a couple of indistinct greenish shapes, show up, they scold their child for playing so roughly, and apologize for his "immature" behavior.

William Campbell, the actor who played Trelane, also appeared as the Klingon commander Captain Koloth in "The Trouble With Tribbles." Campbell found that on Star Trek even the villains could be popular! "I got a tremendous amount of fan mail out of 'The Squire of Gothos.' A lot of people asked me why I didn't get roles like that more often. You know nobody hated me in the end." He got the same sort of response after playing the Klingon captain. "Even the neighborhood kids teased my wife about being 'Mrs. Klingon.'"

There are relatively few completely evil characters in Star Trek. Often the villains are once good people who have somehow become warped. This is certainly true of John Gill in "Patterns of Force." Gill was a distinguished historian and one of Kirk's instructors at Starfleet Academy. But when sent as an undercover observer to the planet Ekos, Gill violates the Prime Directive by introducing an only slightly modified form of Nazism to the planet. Gill is ultimately made the puppet of his own deputy minister, the more evil Melakon.

The episode "Where No Man Has Gone Before" features another of Kirk's early acquaintances who has gone seriously wrong. This time it is Lieutenant Commander Gary Mitchell, Kirk's second in command aboard the *Enterprise* and the captain's oldest friend. Mitchell possesses certain mental powers (called psionic abilities) that allow him to move objects or create illusions. These powers are dormant until the *Enterprise* comes into contact with an extragalactic energy barrier, which both releases his psionic abilities and drives him mad. He begins to think that he is a god who has no responsibility at all to human beings. In the end Kirk is forced to kill his best friend.

A man like James T. Kirk, who has risen rapidly in Starfleet, is bound to have made some enemies along the way. In "Court-Martial" we meet one of them, Lieutenant Commander Benjamin Finney. Finney and Kirk were old friends, in fact Finney named his daughter Jamie for James. But the friends had a falling out over a mistake that Finney had made and that Kirk reported. Kirk's career advanced, and he became captain of the *Enterprise;* Finney's promotion was blocked, and he became only a records officer. He blamed Kirk for this, and his hatred of his former friend grew into an insane obsession. Finney concocts a scheme in which he appears to have been killed through Kirk's negligence, and Kirk faces a court-martial. Jamie first accuses Kirk of murdering her father, but as she begins to realize the truth, she tries to defend him. Jim Kirk often has that sort of an effect on people. Ultimately the scheme is exposed, and Finney suffers a mental and physical breakdown.

Garth of Izar was one of Starfleet's greatest warriors, and a hero of Kirk's from academy days. During one of his more daring exploits Garth was rendered criminally insane as a result of the terrible injuries he received. He was placed on the prison planet Elba II. In his madness Garth has come to believe that he is the master of the universe, far superior to all others, whom he styles as "decadent weaklings." He has acquired the power to change his shape and thus assume the identity of anyone he pleases. In "Whom Gods Destroy," Kirk is momentarily tricked by his old hero but ultimately overcomes the madman. Garth is given the treatment that cures his madness.

While hardly in the class of Garth, Cadet Finnegan was a villain to Jim Kirk while he was still a young man at Starfleet Academy. Finnegan was more of a bully than a true villain, but the torments that he inflicted on Cadet Kirk stuck in his mind. On the amusement park planet, in "Shore Leave," Kirk remembers Cadet Finnegan well enough to materialize his image and gets great satisfaction from punching him out, something he had never been able to do in real life.

Another of Kirk's old classmates gone wrong is R. M. Merik. Merik had dropped out of the academy and become the captain of a commercial space vehicle, the S.S. *Beagle*. But he betrays his crew and turns them over to the cruel rulers of Planet 892-IV, which parallels the old Roman empire, in "Bread and Circuses." For this service Merik is given the title Merikus, First Citizen. He tries to get Kirk to betray the *Enterprise* as he betrayed the *Beagle*. When he fails, he realizes what he has done, tries to make amends, and is killed.

In the Star Trek series there were relatively few episodes in which more than one distinctly nonhumanoid alien appears. Indeed most of the aliens in Star Trek either look quite human or are able to assume human shape. In "Journey to Babel," however, the ambassadors of several different planets are aboard the *Enterprise* on their way to an important peace conference. One of them is Thelev, apparently a young Andorian with the blue skin, white hair, and knobbed antennae typical of that race. He is in reality, however, a disguised Orion spy, out to wreck the conference. Thelev has a transmitting device concealed in his false antennae. He murders Ambassador Gav of Tellar, and tries to pin the crime on Spock's father Sarek of Vulcan.

One of the more unusual guest stars on Star Trek was Melvin Belli, who is not an actor but a well-known and very flamboyant trial attorney.

In "And the Children Shall Lead," he plays Gorgan, who appears first as a vaguely defined, pink-haired humanoid surrounded by a glowing green aura. In reality, while he is still humanoid, he is quite ugly. Gorgan is the last inhabitant of the planet Triacus, and his aim is first to take over the *Enterprise,* and then the Universe. He has tremendous powers, but Kirk is able to resist them, and Gorgan is destroyed. Belli's son, Caesar, also appears in this episode.

In "The Savage Curtain," Kirk and Spock find themselves arrayed against an impressive group of villains. These villains are not "real," they are the creation of Yarnek, a rock creature, and they are to represent the personification of evil, but illusions or not they are still villains. There is Ghenghis Khan, the ruthless, efficient, and successful Mongol conqueror who overran much of Asia in the eleventh century. Allied to the great Khan is Colonel Green, who led a terrifying war on Earth in the early twenty-first century. Green was best known for launching sneak attacks. There is also Kahless, "The Unforgettable," the Klingon who set the pattern for the planet's ruthless tyranny. From the planet Tiburon, Yarnek chooses the warrior woman Zora, who was notorious for performing experiments on subject tribes. Arrayed against this evil quartet are Kirk, Spock, and the images of Abraham Lincoln and Surak, greatest of the Vulcans.

The crew of the *Enterprise* faces a displaced god in "Who Mourns for Adonais?" The ancient Greeks worshiped the god Apollo, but when the *Enterprise* encounters that semi-divine being on the planet Pollux IV, they are not inclined to be worshipful. The problem is that Apollo misses the good old days of being worshiped by peasants. He has exiled himself to that distant planet and then captures the *Enterprise* in the hope of turning the crew into a group of peasant worshipers. When they reject him, he bemoans the ingratitude of humans, and dissolves.

In "Return of the Archons," Kirk and Spock contest with Landru, really an ancient computer containing the stored memory of the scientist who programmed it thousands of years ago. The computer projects the image of a tall, thin, gray-haired man with a soft voice and burning eyes. The computer was supposed to produce a stable society on Beta III, but instead has produced a static and backward one. When Kirk manages to convince Landru that it is harming the people rather than helping them, the computer destroys itself.

* * *

As his name might imply, Kodos the Executioner is a real bad guy. He had been the governor of Tarsus IV, but when food ran short he ordered the execution of half the population in order to allow half to survive. When Federation forces arrived on the planet, they found a burned body that they took to be that of Kodos, and the whole terrible incident seemed ended. But Kodos did not die, he simply changed his identity. He was an excellent actor, and he began calling himself Anton Karidian, leader of an acting troop called the Karidian Players. The *Enterprise* encounters Karidian in "The Conscience of the King," twenty years after he has assumed his new identity. The Karidian Players are performing *Hamlet*. One of the *Enterprise* crew, Lieutenant Kevin Riley, was born on Tarsus IV and lost both his parents to the Executioner. He suspects Karidian's true identity, and wants to kill him. Kirk stops him. As is typical of most Star Trek episodes, the villains are not simple. Karidian's daughter Lenore worships her father and has been secretly killing off all witnesses to the massacre on Tarsus IV. She attempts to kill Kirk, but Karidian is so horrified by what his daughter has done that he steps into the phaser beam aimed at Kirk and dies. Lenore, who is very nearly insane anyway, is driven completely over the edge by this.

* * *

Harcourt Fenton (Harry) Mudd is really more of a rogue than a villain. Liar, thief, and con man, he lives by his wits on the other side of the law. Yet in his dishonest way he is rather lovable—lovable enough to be the center of two Star Trek episodes, "Mudd's Women" and "I, Mudd," a rare honor indeed. In "Mudd's Women" the crew of the *Enterprise* finds Mudd trying to sell three apparently beautiful women to rich husbands. In fact the women have been given a highly illegal drug in order to make them appear beautiful. They are really quite homely. In the end it works out pretty well for the women. Mudd, however, is jailed. But not for long. He turns up again in "I, Mudd," as usual on the run from the law, this time the law of the Denebians, which is very severe. Mudd winds up on a planet inhabited by thousands of too-helpful androids. He is crowned Mudd the First but not allowed to leave. In an attempt to escape he has an android kidnap the *Enterprise*. Then they are all stuck on the planet. Kirk and Mudd are forced into a temporary and uneasy truce by their common predicament. Ultimately the crew of the *Enterprise* is able to confuse and defeat the androids. They escape, leaving Mudd on the planet with the androids, including several hundred replicas of his shrewish wife Stella. Mudd returns once again in the Animated "Mudd's Passion." This time he is peddling a fake love potion, which, to everyone's surprise, turns out to be real. Once again he is sent away for rehabilitation, but no one has much confidence that it will be effective.

Similar in character to Harry Mudd is Cyrano Jones, a somewhat disreputable trader who provides the *Enterprise* with those memorable little beasties, the Tribbles, in "The Trouble With Tribbles." Jones also makes an appearance in the Animated "More Tribbles, More Troubles."

Chapter 10

ALIENS AND ALTERNATE UNIVERSES

The most consistent enemies of the Federation, and thus of the *Enterprise* and her crew, are the Klingons. They have appeared prominently in several Star Trek episodes and in the Star Trek films. The Klingons could never have been considered a good-looking race, but when first encountered in the TV series they were reasonably presentable. On TV the Klingons were rather dark and generally wore small beards and drooping mustaches. Their most prominent features were heavy, upswept eyebrows. Some Klingons, like Captain Koloth, were almost handsome and possessed a certain charm. The years did not improve their appearance or temper, and in the films the Klingons are genuinely grotesque and barbaric. They even speak a guttural language that sounds mean, and in *Star Trek III* we see that their pets are the ugliest-looking, most ill-tempered dogs in the galaxy. Oddly, they have affection for the dogs, though they show little affection for one another.

The Klingon greeting is "survive and succeed." They are a warrior race that comes from a poor planetary system and must colonize and conquer in order to survive. They feel contempt and hatred for all other races, particularly humans. Klingons are constantly warring among themselves and still maintain a tradition of dueling.

The constant hostility between the Federation and the Klingon Empire attracted the attention of a power greater than either, the Organians, who appear to be human but are in reality beings of pure energy. In "Errand of Mercy," the Organians, whose home planet is threatened by the conflict, force the Federation and the Klingons to sign a peace treaty. The treaty provides, in part, that disputed planets go to whichever side can develop them most efficiently, and that the forces of one side may take shore leave at the other's bases. Despite the treaty, there is constant friction, if not outright hostility between the two major galactic powers.

In the films, the Klingons seem almost completely barbaric and evil. But in the TV epi-

Klingons in *Star Trek III*

sodes they sometimes show a side that, while
not precisely lovable, is a bit more "human." In
"The Trouble With Tribbles," a Klingon agent
does try to poison the food supply of an entire
planet, but when Scotty beams the Klingon-
hating Tribbles aboard their spaceship one
can't help but feel a bit sorry for the Klingons.
Tribbles, as the crew of the *Enterprise* discovered, are a great deal of trouble indeed.

The Klingons come off most sympathetically
in "Day of the Dove." In this episode the crew
of the *Enterprise* and the Klingons are driven to
fighting by an insubstantial entity that feeds off
hatred. In order to defeat the entity and save
their own lives, the *Enterprise* crew and the

Klingons must cooperate to starve the entity by ending their fighting and actually laughing the creature out of their ship.

Next to the Klingons, the most persistent enemies of the Federation are the Romulans. They fought a major war with the Federation some one hundred years before the first voyages of the *Enterprise*. A peace treaty was then signed, and an uneasy peace has persisted.

The Romulans are a race closely related to the Vulcans, though they appear to have lost contact with one another before the Vulcans adopted their philosophy of logic. The Romulans themselves are very much warriors, though they are a good deal more noble adversaries than the Klingons; they are better looking, too. The Romulans, however, must have some ties to the Klingons, for Romulan and Klingon ship designs have been exchanged.

Violence is a part of Romulan life. When attacking a ship they customarily take no prisoners. Death is the punishment for disobedience or failure in battle, and death by torture is the Romulan penalty for spying, sabotage, and treason. Yet there is something admirable about the Romulans, who live by a warrior's code. They prefer death to dishonor. Unlike the Klingons, who are completely barbaric, some of the Romulans are highly cultured individuals. Saavik, who is part Romulan, joins the *Enterprise* crew in the films.

One of the great puzzles posed by Star Trek is why so many of the different races encountered throughout the galaxy are humanoid in appearance. Not only are apparently alien races often similar in appearance, but their cultural development appears to be similar as well. For example, in "Bread and Circuses" the obscure Planet 892-IV has developed a Roman-type of empire, complete with Roman names. The observation has led to the formation of Hodgkin's Law of Parallel Planet Development, which holds that cultures tend to develop in similar ways on similar planets. But this law does not satisfactorily explain all of the parallels found throughout the galaxy. In "The Paradise Syndrome," Spock translates the symbols on an ancient obelisk on an Earthlike planet and learns of the Preservers. They are a very advanced race that once traveled throughout the galaxy rescuing primitive cultures in danger of extinction. The Preservers may be the reason behind Hodgkin's Law, and their existence explain why humanoid species are so common in the galaxy. No one knows if the Preservers themselves are humanoid, or if they still exist, for no direct trace of them has ever been found.

The Preservers, it seems, went about meddling with alien cultures. Representatives of the Federation are strictly forbidden to do this by the Prime Directive, also called the Rule of Non-interference or General Order No. 1. The Directive prohibits any sort of interference by the Federation in the normal development of alien life and societies. The Prime Directive can be disregarded under extreme and unusual circumstances, but any Starfleet commander who does so had better be ready to justify his actions fully. In "Return of the Archons," Kirk violates the Directive by interfering directly with the development, or to be more accurate, nondevelopment of culture on Beta III. He argues that the Directive should apply only in the case of healthy cultures, and that on Beta III, under the dead hand of the computer Landru, was by no means a healthy culture. In a number of other episodes Kirk bends, if he does not actually break the Prime Directive; but apparently he has always been fully able to justify his actions.

The U.S.S. *Horizon* visited the planet Iotia before the Prime Directive was established. When the *Horizon* departed, it left behind a book entitled *Chicago Mobs of the Twenties,* a history of the gangsters of Chicago in the 1920s. The humanoid residents of Iotia were very imitative and remade their entire civilization in the image of the Chicago gangs. They used the book on gangs as their Bible. The *Enterprise* arrives a century after the *Horizon* has left and finds a planet ruled by rival gangs who have adapted the clothes, weapons, and speech of old-time Earthly hoods. Kirk and Spock have to try to bring the gang leaders together to work for the good of the entire planet. Though there often is humor in Star Trek, this episode, called "A Piece of the Action," is probably the funniest single episode of all.

In "A Piece of the Action," Kirk invents the most confusing card game in the galaxy, Fizzbin. Here are the rules: Each player gets six cards, except the man on the dealer's right, who gets seven cards. The second card is dealt face up, except on Tuesday. To make the rules somewhat more confusing Kirk deals all the cards face up during the explanation. Two jacks is half a fizzbin, but three jacks is a sralk and disqualifies the player. One needs a king or a deuce, except at night when a queen or a four will do. If another jack is dealt that's good unless the card on the next deal is a six, in which case the player has to give back one card. However, if the six is a black six then the player gets an additional card. The object is to get a royal fizzbin, but the odds against that are beyond calculation. The real object of the game is to confuse and distract the two hoods with whom Kirk is playing cards. If simple confusion isn't enough there is always the kronk. That's when the dealer deliberately drops a card, and when the player leans over to pick it up the dealer knocks the table over on him and a general fight follows.

Isis, who appears sometimes as a black cat wearing a diamond necklace, and briefly as a beautiful, black-haired woman wearing the same necklace, is possibly a member of an advanced race that has no qualms at all about meddling with the development of primitive cultures. When in "Assignment Earth" the *Enterprise* goes back in time to find out how Earth managed to survive the violent and dangerous twentieth century, Kirk and company meet Gary Seven, who claims to be a twentieth-century Earthman trained by an advanced race to prevent the people of the Earth from destroying themselves. The motives of these aliens in attempting to manipulate Earth history are unknown but are assumed to be good, for Earth did indeed survive.

The longest-running race war in the galaxy was on the planet Cheron. In "Let That Be Your Last Battlefield," the *Enterprise* intercepts a shuttlecraft stolen from Starbase 4. Aboard is Lokai, who is fleeing a charge of treason on Cheron. He has been on the run for some fifty thousand years. He is being pursued by Bele, chief officer of the Commission of Political Traitors. The dispute between the two aliens is basically a racial one. Lokai is a representative of a race that is white on the right side of its face and black on the left. Bele, on the other hand, is from a race that is black on the right side and white on the left. For reasons known only to the aliens (and perhaps not even to them), the coloring has given Bele's people supremacy over Lokai's people. Both talk in clichés about racial equality and inequality, and there is no real dialogue between the two. Kirk returns the warring pair to their home planet of Cheron. But Cheron is now a lifeless world, the inhabitants of the planet having destroyed themselves in a race war. Both Lokai and Bele beam down to the planet where they will fight the final battle of their age-old war on the surface of a world destroyed by their hatred.

In "Mirror Mirror" the *Enterprise* encounters not an alien world but an alternate, or mirror, universe. In a sense, everything in this alternate universe looks the same but is backward. Kirk, Scott, McCoy, and Uhura are thrown into the mirror universe while being transported during an ion storm. Their counterparts appear in the "normal" universe. In the mirror universe the Federation is replaced by

Ilia

the Galactic Empire, dominated by fear and force. The Imperial Starship *Enterprise* is ruled by assassination and conspiracy. What is most fascinating about this particular episode is that it probes each of the main characters and shows how their opposites might behave. Kirk-2 from the mirror universe is a killer who assumed control of the *Enterprise* by assassinating Captain Pike. McCoy-2 is a sadist who runs his sick bay like a torture chamber. Chekov-2 is an assassin who tries to kill his captain. All the rest of the *Enterprise* crew from the mirror universe are equally rotten. Only Spock-2 is relatively unchanged, though he is harder and colder than his "normal" counterpart. In this universe, are the Klingons the good guys? We don't know.

In *Star Trek: The Motion Picture* there appear to be more aliens serving on the crew of the *Enterprise,* but few of them figure importantly in the story. One who does is Lieutenant Ilia, the beautiful, though totally bald native of Delta V. *Star Trek II* introduces an even more interesting alien, Saavik, half-Vulcan, half-Romulan, and completely formidable. She also appears in *Star Trek III* and survives the breakup of the Genesis planet. Whether Saavik will become a regular of the Star Trek company only time will tell.

Saavik

Chapter 11

THE FILMS

The script for *Star Trek: The Motion Picture* was written by Gene Roddenberry, and the film was directed by Robert Wise, who had directed *The Sound of Music,* but also such science fiction classics as *The Day the Earth Stood Still* and *The Andromeda Strain*.

While real Star Trek fans loved the film, some noted that the plot was very similar to three episodes of the TV series: "The Immunity Syndrome," in which the *Enterprise* must penetrate to the center of a mysterious energy cloud; "The Doomsday Machine," in which the *Enterprise* meets an immense device that destroys entire planets; and most particularly "The Changeling," in which the *Enterprise* encounters an alien-rebuilt space probe, Nomad, which now possesses tremendous powers and has come back looking for its creator. Some joked that the film should be called "Where Nomad Has Gone Before."

Like the TV series itself, *Star Trek: The Motion Picture* is not just another space opera or big-budget galactic shoot-'em-up. There is plenty of adventure, but there are also ideas, and there are characters. That's why some adventure film fans think the picture is slow. One of the major themes is Spock finally recognizing his own humanity. He makes the startling admission "Logic and knowledge are not enough."

Kolinahr is the Vulcan ceremony in which an individual is purged of all emotions. As *Star Trek: The Motion Picture* opens, Spock has been undergoing that ceremony. When he first appears he is colder, more emotionless than ever. He is almost zombie-like. But he has stopped the process of Kolinahr before it is finished in order to return to the *Enterprise,* because he is seeking something.

Star Trek: The Motion Picture ends with the words "The human adventure is just beginning."

The inspiration for *Star Trek II: The Wrath of Khan* was the TV episode "Space Seed," in which Khan is first introduced. When Khan and his cohorts are deposited on the remote

Spock's father in *Star Trek III*

and rugged planet Ceti Alpha V, Kirk wonders what will happen twenty years later. That episode was first aired early in 1967. The film was released in June of 1982. Kirk didn't have to wait a full twenty years to find out.

Chosen to direct *Star Trek II* was young Nicholas Meyer, a writer turned director who had already directed an excellent but relatively unappreciated science fiction film, *Time After Time*. Meyer went on to direct the searing TV film *The Day After*, about the results of a nuclear war. *The Day After* was the most watched TV movie in history. Meyer said, "I've never had any desire to do a film about spaceships. I did have a desire to make a movie about the people aboard them, however." Just about everyone agrees that Meyer did a brilliant job with this film, and though it is technically very impressive, it is also mainly about people (and Vulcans).

Rumor soon got out that Spock was to be killed in *Star Trek II*. Actually, in the first draft of the film Spock was killed in the middle of the story, not at the end, and much of the film was to be taken up with the relationship between Kirk and Saavik, first conceived of as a male Vulcan. Fans were outraged. Those who had started a save Star Trek letter-writing campaign now began a save Spock letter-writing campaign. Some fans took out an ad in *Variety*, the Hollywood trade paper, saying that if Spock were killed they would boycott the film, and the studio would lose millions.

There were all sorts of rumors about why Spock was to be killed. Those who worked on the film were very secretive about what was supposed to happen, and the film was shot under unusually tight security. But when the fans saw the ending of *Star Trek II*, they realized that while Spock was dead, his death was only temporary. In practically all other Star Trek stories the closing narration is spoken by Kirk. In the film the closing words are those of Spock.

* * *

Spock brought back to life in *Star Trek III*

There was only one major cast change for *Star Trek III*. The part of Saavik, which had been played very successfully by Kirstie Alley, was taken by Robin Curtis. That upset some fans, but Saavik was a newcomer, not a longtime crew member from TV days. Otherwise all the regulars were back, including Leonard Nimoy, not only as Spock but as the director of the film.

The very distinguished actress Dame Judith Anderson makes a brief but memorable appearance as T'Lar, the Vulcan high priestess.

Yeoman Janice Rand (played by Grace Lee Whitney, who was a regular during Star Trek's first TV season) makes a brief cameo appearance in *Star Trek III*. She is one of the people sitting in an observation lounge when the battered *Enterprise* docks near Earth. This film also gives us our first extended look at Earth in the twenty-third century, including a look at Kirk's elegant San Francisco apartment.

The scientific research vessel *Grissom* is named after the twentieth-century American astronaut Gus Grissom, who was killed in a launch-pad fire while testing the Apollo spacecraft.

When information leaked out that *Star Trek III* would end with the destruction of the *Enterprise*, many fans were upset. Some threatened to boycott the film, just as they had threatened to boycott *Star Trek II* if Spock were killed. In the end, most of them went anyway, and left with the hope that there would be a new *Enterprise* in future films.

Chapter 12

THE FANS

No television series in history has ever had more loyal, dedicated, and effective fans than Star Trek. The depth of fan devotion came as a surprise even to those who had helped to make the show. When, after the end of the first TV season, there were rumors that the show was to be canceled, the fans flooded NBC with letters. When, at the end of the second season, the network announced that the show definitely would be canceled, the flood of mail increased to the point where the network was forced to change its decision. Other TV shows have since been saved from cancellation by letter-writing campaigns, but the outpouring for Star Trek was unprecedented. The fans also kept up the pressure for the return of Star Trek that ultimately resulted in the continuing series of Star Trek films.

NBC executives who wanted to cancel Star Trek always suspected that executive producer Gene Roddenberry had organized the massive save Star Trek letter-writing campaign. But while Roddenberry was certainly not displeased with the support for his series, it was really a grass-roots movement. The real leader was a fan named Bjo (pronounced Bee-jo) Trimble. She had been involved in Star Trek fandom from the start and knew a lot of other people who were, too. She helped to begin the campaign, advise people about what sort of letters to write and where to send them, and contact various fan organizations to encourage them to write letters. She had at first planned a fairly small-scale campaign, but it mushroomed, and the results surprised even Bjo. NBC received somewhere around one million save Star Trek letters. No one is sure of the exact number. The mailroom at NBC was swamped. After NBC announced on the air that the show would be returned for a third season, the mailroom was swamped again. This time with thank-you letters.

Practically every form of entertainment has its own devoted group of fans. Science fiction fans are more devoted than most, and Star Trek fans the most devoted of all. Fan, by the way, is short for fanatic—and that is appropriate for

Star Trek fandom. A devoted fan will collect videotapes, books, magazines, photographs, autographs, old props, practically anything related even remotely to Star Trek. Fans also publish their own magazines, called fanzines, devoted entirely to Star Trek. Fans read and review other fanzines and write and call one another regularly. For some it is an important part of their lives. The result is an organized network of people around the country devoted to Star Trek. In fact, Star Trek has fans all over the world. It is particularly popular in Japan.

Hard-core Star Trek fans are generally called Trekkies—though some prefer being called Trekkers and are offended if you call them Trekkies. There is a subgroup that is interested only in Spock. They are called Spockies.

Trekkies are experts on the series. They can answer questions like, What was Spock's mother's maiden name? It was Grayson.

Fanzines contain reviews of new Star Trek movies and books, news about forthcoming Star Trek projects, and news of the doings of the stars like Shatner and Nimoy. They report on the activities of other fan groups. There are also long articles on different aspects of the Star Trek universe, for example on the weapons or on Captain Kirk's family history. If the reproduction allows it there are drawings. But perhaps the most interesting part of many fanzines is the fan-written Star Trek stories. The fans use the basic Star Trek characters and situations and create their own fiction. Some of it is bad, some good, and some just plain strange. But to be a true Trekkie (or Trekker) requires more than simply watching all the TV episodes and movies and remembering a lot of details. It requires real involvement.

Fanzines often have funny names. Here are a few of them: *Terran Times, Spock's Showcase, Anti-Matter, Nimoyan Digest, The William Shatner Letter, Log of the U.S.S.* Enterprise, *Overload* (a publication devoted to Scotty), *Quadrant, Starfleet Communications,* and *Spockanalia.* Most publications like these survive for only a few issues, sometimes only one. They come out very irregularly. But when one dies there always seems to be another to take its place.

Star Trek fans often hold conventions, some quite small and local, others huge. A 1976 convention at a New York hotel attracted some thirty thousand people and lots of newspaper and television coverage. Though Star Trek regulars may appear at the conventions to speak, the conventions themselves are not directly connected to Star Trek. Sometimes those who have organized the conventions have been incompetent and have not delivered what they promised. A few convention promoters have been accused of being downright dishonest and misappropriating funds. But for the most part these gatherings are just plain fun. Trekkies are a prominent feature of most general science fiction conventions as well.

One of the most popular parts of any convention is the screening of a "blooper reel." These are made up of scenes that were cut because somebody forgot a line, or a prop didn't work, or there was some other sort of goof-up. Bloopers are inevitable in making a television show or a movie, but the Star Trek bloopers are funnier than those from most other shows. Maybe that's because the cast is usually so good-humored that when something goes wrong they begin to laugh, too. Pretty soon everyone in the audience is laughing along with those on the screen.

Fans campaigned to have President Gerald Ford name the first U.S. space shuttlecraft *Enterprise*. Even NASA officials were surprised when he did. As the shuttle was rolled out for its first public viewing at Edwards Air Force Base in California, the band played the Star Trek theme. One of the senators who spoke at the ceremony quipped that none of the astronauts were really qualified to fly the craft because they didn't have pointy ears.

* * *

Star Trek is the basis for a variety of video games, from arcade games to those designed for the home computer. Most of the games are fairly simple. The player sits at the controls of the *Enterprise* and zaps attacking Klingon ships. Some, however, are extremely complex. Not only must the player fight off attacking Klingons, he or she must move characters throughout the ship, put out fires or make other repairs when necessary, even replace characters that have been injured or killed. Writer David Gerrold reported that he was so upset when he accidentally killed Dr. McCoy during one game he has been unable to play it since.

In large numbers Star Trek fans can at times be a little too admiring. Shatner, Nimoy, and others have all found themselves nearly trampled at one time or another. DeForest Kelley remembers going to see a play and being mobbed by fans in the lobby when he was recognized. It took all the ushers and security men in the theater to get him out safely. "That was the first time I was ever mobbed, and it was completely shocking," he said. On a promotional tour Leonard Nimoy found that the same girl called him in his hotel room in every city he went to. Somehow she had gotten hold of his complete itinerary. But most of the Star Trek regulars appreciate the fan support and admiration, just as long as it doesn't get out of hand. "It's rather a singular privilege to be placed on a pedestal like this," says George Takei.

Gene Roddenberry had a unique way of honoring the contributions of Star Trek's fans. When *Star Trek: The Motion Picture* was made, more than one hundred and fifty leading fans were cast as crew members of the *Enterprise*. They were also given a free meal and paid a day as extras. Said one fan, "I'd have paid *them!*"

STAR TREK

TRIVIA QUIZ

1. In what year did Star Trek first begin on television?
   A) 1962   B) 1966   C) 1971   D) 1974

2. What actor was first scheduled to play the captain of the *Enterprise?*
   A) Gene Roddenberry   B) William Shatner
   C) Jeffrey Hunter   D) Ricardo Montalban

3. How many episodes of the original Star Trek TV series were made?
   A) 64   B) 71   C) 79   D) 87

4. What was the title of the last regular Star Trek episode shown on network TV?
   A) "The Menagerie"   B) "Turnabout Intruder"   C) "Let This Be Your Last Battlefield"   D) "The Wrath of Khan"

5. Where was James T. Kirk born?
   A) Iowa   B) San Francisco   C) Florida
   D) Canada

6. When Kirk was a Starfleet cadet he idolized:
   A) Garth of Izar   B) Gary Mitchell   C) Cadet
   Finnegan   D) Colonel Green

7. Spock's father is named:
   A) Saavik   B) Persis Khambatta   C) Sar-
   gon   D) Sarek

8. The Vulcan mating urge is called:
   A) T'Lar   B) T'Pring   C) pon farr
   D) Ahn-woon

9. Before Star Trek, William Shatner and Leonard
   Nimoy appeared together in:
   A) "The Lieutenant"   B) "The Brothers Ka-
   ramazov"   C) "Outer Limits"   D) "The
   Man from U.N.C.L.E."

10. Dr. McCoy has a daughter named:
    A) Nancy   B) Kelley   C) Joanna   D) Nichelle

11. Before Star Trek, James Doohan, who plays
    Scotty, worked extensively:
    A) in radio   B) in films   C) on television
    D) on the stage

12. Sulu is an expert:
   A) at the martial arts   B) tennis player
   C) fencer   D) chess player

13. Lieutenant Uhura's name means freedom in
   which language?
   A) German   B) Vulcan   C) Latin   D) Swahili

14. Chekov is the *Enterprise*'s . . .
   A) navigator   B) helmsman   C) transporter
   chief   D) first lieutenant

15. Nurse Chapel is hopelessly in love with:
   A) Spock   B) Kirk   C) Chekov   D) Decker

16. Majel Barrett, who plays Nurse Chapel, is mar-
   ried to:
   A) Kevin Riley   B) Leonard Nimoy   C) Gene
   Roddenberry   D) John Wayne

17. The Tribbles are sold by:
   A) Gary Mitchell   B) Harry Mudd
   C) Cyrano Jones   D) John Gill

18. The Planet 892-IV has a civilization which par-
   allels:
   A) old Chicago   B) ancient China   C) the
   American Indians   D) the Roman Empire

19. An invisibility screen was developed by:
    A) the Klingons B) the Romulans C) the
    Vulcans D) the Federation

20. Which of these characters has been played by
    two different actors.
    A) Saavik B) Kirk C) Chekov D) Dr.
    M'Benya.

21. What is Kirk holding?

22. On what planet does Spock assume the disguise of a Nazi?

Answers:
1-B; 2-C; 3-C; 4-B; 5-A; 6-A; 7-D; 8-C; 9-D; 10-C; 11-A; 12-C; 13-D; 14-A; 15-A; 16-C; 17-C; 18-D; 19-B; 20-A; 21-Tribbles; 22-Ekos.

Scoring:

21-22—Admiral	6-10—Plebe
16-20—Captain	0-5—Klingon Spy
11-15—Cadet	

ABOUT THE AUTHOR

DANIEL COHEN is the author of over a hundred books for both young readers and adults, including some titles he has co-authored with his wife SUSAN. Among their popular titles are: *Supermonsters; The Greatest Monsters in the World; Real Ghosts; Ghostly Terrors; Science Fiction's Greatest Monsters; The World's Most Famous Ghosts; The Monsters of Star Trek; The Kid's Guide to Home Computers; Rock Video Superstars;* and *Wrestling Superstars,* all of which are available in Archway Paperback editions.

A former managing editor of *Science Digest* Magazine, Mr. Cohen was born in Chicago and has a degree in journalism from the University of Illinois. He appears frequently on radio and television, and has lectured at colleges and universities throughout the country. He lives with his wife, young daughter, one dog and four cats in Port Jervis, New York.

141

Sports Illustrated

AND ARCHWAY PAPERBACKS
BRING YOU
GREAT MOMENTS IN FOOTBALL AND BASEBALL

<u>Sports Illustrated</u>, America's most widely-read sports magazine, and Archway Paperbacks have joined forces to bring you some of the most exciting and amazing moments in football and baseball.

GREAT MOMENTS IN PRO FOOTBALL
Bill Gutman
Here are the amazing stories of passes that looked impossible, broken records that seemed untouchable and many other spectacular moments.

STRANGE AND AMAZING FOOTBALL STORIES
Bill Gutman
Read about the incredible catches and the bizarre once-in-a-lifetime flukes that make the gridiron the unpredictable place it is.

Coming in Spring 1987

GREAT MOMENTS IN BASEBALL
Bill Gutman
As spring training approaches you will be able to enjoy this exciting book full of great performances, close plays and super team efforts.

STRANGE AND AMAZING BASEBALL STORIES
Bill Gutman
Don't miss the zany, unbelievable and mysterious happenings past and present in the world of baseball.